MW01251637

Printed in the United States of America

First Printing, May 2019

ISBN 978-0-359-63852-9

Lulu Press Incorporated

627 Davis Drive, Suite 300
Morrisville, NC 27650
www.lulu.com

We're all pretty bizarre, some of us are just better at hiding it, that's all

— Andrew Clark,
The breakfast Club

Just a Little Note

I don't like not knowing. So even the idea of not knowing how my life will end gives me anxiety. I've been told so many times that I overthink things - every little word people say, every little thing they do. Therefore, to save your time and the money you are about to spend on this book, I should say that this book has no ending; life doesn't end. It's in a constant state of growth and just like life, I am in constant growth. It doesn't matter what you are going through, doesn't matter if you have more on your plate than the person next to you on the bus or in your favourite coffeehouse. Everybody will reach their own end point in their own particular way, and we'll all find that happy ending people keep talking about. But the truth is, those are nothing but temporary happy endings. Troubles don't bid you adieu simply because you feel you are done with them and you think you've reached your true destination of bliss. There is always more to worry about. This book talks about my fair share of troubles, drama, sentiments and emotions that shaped me into the person I am today. I've found that after a while, you get tired of questioning why people left the way they did. You keep thinking how easy it would be to just bury the memories and escape it all. If you decide to read this, then welcome to my life. I urge you to take mental notes as to not repeat my mistakes. If not, if you feel too judgemental or too busy with your life, just put the book down because I don't think this would be good for you.

> P. S. The songs suggested to listen to at the top of couple of pages are the ones that I listened while I wrote that part.

INNER THOUGHT #1

Me before today

I don't really remember when I first found myself interested in drama. It's like I always knew, like it's always been a part of me.

When I was younger - maybe about three or four - I first fell in love with acting and theatre. My mom would video tape me and I would act as just about everything; a painter, a teacher, even a cook. It was always so fun to leave the actual world behind, even for a mere few moments, and imagine another version of my life, another version of myself.

I had a complicated childhood. Maybe that's the root of my current personal complexities, who knows. I mean, my mom got married at age eighteen and had me when she was only twenty years old. And my dad was never there, emotionally or physically. Whatever memories I have of him now are all in that dark, dusty part of my mind that I'd rather never visit again. Those tunnels are filled with pieces of me that I'm afraid to let resurface.

When I started elementary school, like anyone else I wanted to find good friends. I was quite good at it at the time. Always a leader, I craved the thrill of being in charge and took any chance to be the boss.

I think it was the summer after second grade that I joined a choir group at some sort of camp near my house. I remember that was the first time I tried to write a piece, and the teacher told me that I really suck at it. That was the first time someone said anything at all about my writing, and, well, it wasn't the last time.

But it was enough to make me give up on writing, thinking I would never be good enough. And I seemed to do so much better in choir, so I just focused on that for a while.

When I started fourth grade, I wanted to do more than choir, so I joined the basketball team. And from there I thought, *Oh, classical music and piano... that's what's for me.* I thought I found my true self, but how foolish I was. That was so far away from who I really am.

By the end of the year, I'd left both choir and basketball, and from fifth grade on I immersed myself in school and forced myself to focus on getting good grades.

In August of the summer before sixth grade, my grandpa passed away. My mom's father. With my mom lost in grief and no one else to lean on, I felt lonely. For the first time ever, I thought that I was completely alone, and I thought I would never get my mom back. Meanwhile at school, I started hanging out with kids who were nothing but bad influences on me. My grades began to slip as I started caring less and less about school, and things just got bad. The same group of people I thought were my friends called me stupid among other things, and, well, I let them. It's like intentionally or unintentionally, I let people hurt me in the worst ways possible. The rest is a blur but all I can say is that it was a very bad year.

Second year of middle school, the seventh grade, was a blast. Good friends, good company and amazing memories. But knowing my life, I never stay somewhere long enough to call it home. We moved, right after that year. And by the time I started eighth grade, everything was new: our house, my school, maybe even me.

It would take a whole book to describe whatever it was that happened that year, but to summarize, it was a bittersweet experience; I was used and abused very badly on an emotional level.

Honestly, to this day, seven years later, there are still lots of missing pieces of that puzzle that I myself can't put together, and that's okay. Some things are meant to be felt, not told.

And life moves on, yet that was how my story started.

She was just a butterfly
Wandering from branch to branch
Learning how to fly...

INNER THOUGHT #2

It is a fine morning in September. Or it was, until I hear my alarm clock go off - God, how that sound ignites such pain in me every morning, I'll never understand. I try to reach for my phone on the nightstand while my eyes are still closed. As I'm reaching, my hand suddenly gets wet, and that's when I remember the glass of water, I had with me last night. I hear my mom shout, "Hurry up, hon! You don't want to be late for your first day!"

I eventually manage to drag myself out of bed, my feet touching the cold floor; I figure my mom had opened the window when she woke up. The chilly breeze of early morning is everywhere. The smell of fresh bread wafts out of the oven, mixed with my mom's famous perfume that she always wears. She opens her arms trying to give me a hug, but I just stare right through her, shaking my head. Despite the fact that her hugs are my favourite thing in the world, the most comfortable place ever, I want no part of it today. Today, I'm nervous and she knows it. So, I retreat to my room.

I hear her leave as the door closes harshly with the force of the wind, or maybe it's just my nerves. I don't know if it's the insecurities or if it's just me being extra, but it takes trying on ten outfits for me to be satisfied enough to head out the door. I look in the mirror, saying to myself, "This year is going be amazing for you. You won't even remember the stupid drama of last year." *I really hope so*, I think as I close the door and walk away, ready to make those words a reality for once.

I'm on my way to school when suddenly I see an old friend passing the street. She is of average height, has curly black hair, and dark eyes. I guess you could say that she is pretty on the outside, but her inside needs a bit of redecoration (well, in my opinion, at least). Bumping into her was not my intention, not today. So, I start slowly walking towards the school, trampling the dead orange leaves on the ground; I can hear the sound of my steps as I'm walking, as if it's the only sound in the world.

The weather is delightful today. The enchanting atmosphere of a September morning, the cool breeze on my skin. But I can't even appreciate it because as I'm walking towards the school, I'm focusing just on keeping myself out of her sight. It usually takes fifteen minutes to get to school from my house, but today the streets somehow seem longer, and my steps seem shorter than usual. Maybe the thought of seeing them is harder than I thought it would be.

It takes a long time to find my homeroom, but it takes even longer to find the courage to go in. Somehow, I find myself in the classroom I dreaded, and I glance around to see if I know anyone. And there he is, in his light grey t-shirt, with his black leather jacket on top. How can a person be both so familiar and strange at the same time? I can feel him looking at me, his gaze weighing heavily upon me. I can hear him whispering something, but I don't know if these sounds are coming from him or if they're just made up in my head. At this point, I'm so lost in my thoughts that I almost don't hear my teacher tell me to sit down. I quickly find a spot and sit down in the first pair of desks in the middle column. If I wasn't nervous this morning, I am now. I can feel the hotness in my cheeks; I sense them turning scarlet. I feel sweat running down my face and get up to grab a napkin and clean it up. But that does not make me feel any better. As I'm standing in the corner of the classroom, near the door, I can smell him. I feel his breath as he asks:

"Is everything okay?"

There he was again - the guy that I thought was my one and only. You see, last year when I was new to both the school and the city, I met him in my sophomore science class. He was this hippie kid with the most amazing smile. Those are the ones you need to fear the most. And me, who promised to never fall again after what happened back in Montreal, fell for him with the first words that came out of his mouth. I remember how psyched I was and how I told my friend, Stella, later that day in Civics that I have a huge crush on him. Well, I guess you could say I was lucky that year because just one week later, he told me that he liked me back. And, a week after, we started dating.

Today, as he asks if I'm okay, I shake my head, but I think my eyes are selling me out. I gaze up at him, totally mute. He touches my arm, rubbing his hand on my shoulder trying to comfort me. Damn, he still remembers how to calm me down. We haven't talked in what feels like a lifetime and being in the same room as him makes me so tense. And right here, right now, it feels like just he and I. A wave of nausea overcomes me and I start biting my lip. I'm pretty sure I started shivering about 20 seconds ago. We are making full eye contact. I start touching my necklace, rubbing it in my hand absentmindedly. I take a deep breath. He is still looking directly into my eyes. My shivering has turned into a soft vibration now. I just need to say one word. One single word and then I can go. I can be free from this tension. But it's like I can't say anything, like my mind doesn't want to let me breathe. This is the time to do what I always do. So, I slowly ask the teacher if I can be excused.

And I run away. Literally. I don't even wait to hear the answer. I open the door without fully turning, feeling the cold doorknob on my sweaty hand, and turn it. I almost fall from leaning against it, and I think to myself that the door does what anyone else I've ever tried to lean on does: it betrays my trust. I make my way towards the bathroom, turning around a thousand times to make sure he is not following me. Then I push the door so hard that I almost hit a girl. I try so hard to force the apology out of my mouth, but I'm too late as she's already

gone by the time the words escape my lips. As I reach the fountain and pour several handfuls of water on my face, my mascara is running.

I walk towards the mirror. Seeing myself is almost scary; I look like a ghost. Standing there, staring at my own reflection, I wonder how I could possibly survive a full semester of this tension and anxiety.

That's when my mind tracks back to him. He's probably confused because I totally ignored him in the hallway and now, he's wondering why. This past summer, he'd texted me saying how sorry he was for breaking up with me that way. And, well, I did accept the apology, so we should be fine. We should be talking, right? But for me, this is all so weird because I can't act like nothing ever happened between us. I can't erase the past. I don't want to erase it, I just want to live with it. I'm trying to live with it.

That was my first anxiety attack, or the first one I can remember. I didn't know it at the time, at least not until it had already passed. It always passes.

I make my way to the second period - law class. That is where I see you. You, who used to call me "bestie." Before each other, we'd both been hurt too many times to believe in best friends. But we built the friendship. A friendship I cherished and cared for day after day. A friendship I swore on my life I'd hold onto. One that I thought would last forever. But I guess life is not that predictable after all. Because today, after almost two years, we don't see eye to eye anymore, and my heart aches thinking about old times. But I don't miss you anymore, or him, or anyone who isn't in my life anymore; I just simply miss what I had with them. I will always miss having that special someone.

Life is too short to get stuck in the past and whatever it stands for. No matter the experience, it truly shaped the person I am today. And I'm thankful.

INNER THOUGHT #3.

"Stop This Train" by John Mayer

It's weird when I think about how we could all just be pretending. What does it really mean to be truly happy? Well, for starters, I'm pretty sure that happiness is directly proportional to your expectations. Those little competitions you face every day of your life. Everybody will feel broken into a million pieces at some point in life. Everyone is going to feel pain in their hearts, and everyone is going to experience that pain in a different way. After all, everyone values things differently than others.

It's funny, how life just continues with or without you. It's exactly liked the bus, or the train, or any other kind of transportation, really. They all continue according to the schedule; no return engagement, no encores. And me, I find it hard to believe that people who have left you will miss you eventually. I know they won't. They will regret their decisions, sure, but that doesn't necessarily mean they will miss you. When we first moved to Montreal, everything seemed so hard and almost impossible to achieve. This wasn't because I couldn't speak French, or because I was only fourteen. It was the thought of having to leave everything behind that terrified me. It still does. But as I said, life doesn't wait for you to adjust yourself. It moves on. Therefore, I had to do it, too.

I'm your fundamental hopeless romantic. I love easily, and I care too much. I believe all those embarrassing and idiotic moments are all part of the person I am today. Every time that you engage with someone, from sparing a minute at the bus stop to spending minutes of every day with that person - they will affect you. Back in Montreal, I thought I'd found my very first love. It was just like the movies; meet in school, like each other from the moment you meet, and then live happily ever after. But while I truly have faith in that there is a place where each and every one of us belongs, "fairy tales" and "happily ever after" don't exist. That year, I didn't choose the person I fell in love with; you never do.

Pure Imagination

"Six feet under" by Billie Eilish

It's really hard to look at someone
and listen to their heart at the same time.
Not everybody is capable of doing so
(at least I know I'm usually not).
I can never tell if you're lying,
I can't tell if you're playing games,
I can't tell if you're making fun of me,
I can't really tell if you're being serious.
But I will know when you're sad.
I will notice when you need me there,
and I will know when to give you some space.
But wait a second -
you don't even want me.
You want her,
you need her,
you think you can't really live without her.
I'm here,
listening to your nonsense about her,
and thinking about what's wrong with me that
you can't see me.
You can't look at me
and have those spacious spheres eyes shining.
The way they turn when you talk about her -
I never had someone like that.
Never experienced two-way,
true true love.
I know everybody says that
but they all have someone
at the end of the day.

Everybody has someone but me.
I'm always alone,
always lonely with my thoughts.
My thoughts are like my prison
And right now you are my hour break in the prison
yard. 'Cause when I'm with you,
I zone out.
I become this four-year-old kid
that can't stop staring at you,
can't stop thinking about those lips, those eyes,
can't stop imagining about kissing you
and having my fingers going slowly through your hair,
can't stop imagining how good you might smell
when you're holding me in your arms
and saying that you will never let me go.
But what a shame -
'cause that is all nothing but pure imagination.

INNER THOUGHT #4

"The Only Exception" by Paramore

Sometimes in life, you bump into a rock down the road. Despite its size, you should know that it will guide you towards a better version of yourself. I know that's everyone says, and I also know that it's hard to accept that truth.

I think a lot about all those moments that I was pushed down. All those 'no's and those 'you are not good enough's. They are meant to teach you a lesson, but if not truly guided, you, the over-thinker with the golden heart, might have trouble understanding their true meaning. You might never get up again. Sometimes, it's hard to be strong, and that's okay. But strength is as easy as walking can be. You have to start with baby steps, slow and steady. Then you can walk faster and faster day by day.

I was only four when my parents got separated, and ten when they finally got the divorce. I went back and forth between them for ages, watched them fight over me. Saw my mom struggle in the jungle full of wolves trying to make my life the best it could be. As for my dad, I used to love him. He was kind and caring. Before everything fell apart. He got sick. Sick of life, sick of me - so he stopped trying. By age nine, I barely saw him anymore. One Saturday night, he took me to his brother's house, left for a cigarette, and never came back.

I don't really like talking about this, or him. I sometimes question the way I feel about him. I feel bad for not reaching out now that I'm older. For not wanting to do anything with him. But then I remember all the nightmares that haunted my soul throughout my childhood. The ones that still plague me from time to time. And I carry on, without him. I know his addiction wasn't a choice, but not making the choice to quit and get better is what made me feel so small. He left me and created this big black hole in my heart that will never be fixed. Girls need a father just as much as a mother to rely on.

Ted Mosby said once in *How I Met Your Mother*: "If you're looking for the word that means caring about someone beyond all rationality and wanting them to have everything, they want no matter how much it destroys you, it's love. And when you love someone you just, you...you don't stop, ever. Even when people roll their eyes and call you crazy. Even then. Especially then. You just—you don't give up. Because if I could just give up...if I could just, you know, take the whole world's advice and—and move on and find someone else, that wouldn't be love. That would be... that would be some other disposable thing that is not worth fighting for. But I—that's not what this is."

I'm tired of people saying they know me
when they actually don't.
They don't know about my sleepless nights,
they don't know that most of the time
I cry myself to sleep.
They don't know how it feels to be me.
I'm not saying nobody else had any problems -
 I'm saying everybody has it differently,
but some have it easier than others.
Some have a decent home
and decent parents.
And if they don't,
they have decent friends growing up.
I had none of those.
My dad was an alcoholic,
a cocaine addict.
I had no mom who was just there
'cause being a mom was all that she needed to be.   My
dad left me one day
and never came back for his daughter.
No, I didn't have an easy childhood -
I had a messed-up family,
I had messed up friendship,
I had myself teaching me how to live,
and my books
and my favourite teddy bear
who knew all the secrets,
knew all the emotions I wasn't brave enough
to share with anyone else.
I can't ever tell anyone how sad I am

or how jealous the little things make me.
I can't handle jokes, I take them too seriously.
 People made fun of me,
pushed me into the little corner of my mind,
that dark place that nobody has ever been,
and they left me there.
They say physical bullying is the worst
because it hurts the most.
But what hurts the most are words.
The way someone makes a sentence,
the way someone reacts towards you,
the way someone demonstrates their opinion,
those are the things that matter.
To me, sadly, every single opinion matters,
and that is why I try so hard to look nice every day.
I'm scared of people
judging me with their googly eyes.
Mankind is not kind,
it's selfish.
They don't care if they hurt you,
or about that tiny little word they said
or about that tiny little thing they did.
They don't care that it might follow you
like a shadow
step
by
step
for the rest of your life.
People think I'm easy to read,
just like an open book
yet nobody knows me
deeply.

Nobody dares to get to know that side of me.
Everybody walks away before they get too close.
It's like that dark haunted pathway
in the middle of nowhere
with no lights
or anything for that matter to guide you,
and nobody will ever go
so, no one will never know
all the secrets I keep,
all the dreams that haunt me
every night before I sleep.
Instead they'll leave me all alone,
floating in the air.
And I don't really know
where this air will take me next.

INNER THOUGHT #5

"Summer Love" by Drake

Maybe I am that shy and awkward friend who people talk to just to get to the best friend. That's how it used to be before and maybe it still is. I never truly felt included. Never felt like I was part of something big, part of the crowd. Like I can be whoever I want to be. I just want to feel the acceptance, feel the love.

"Strawberries and Cigarettes" by Troye Sivan

I crave that friendship in *Love, Simon*. It points out how imperfectly perfect a friendship can be. It shows that you have to appreciate every little thing that is currently happening in your life. The funny car rides, singing 2000s throw-back songs at the top of your lungs. The drunken nights where you can barely walk and the lazy mornings where you don't want to leave your bed.
Everybody experiences some basic things, some tough and some tougher, nothing's easy. But it's awfully nice to experience things with people that you deeply care about. Because there's so much beauty in the naked versions of ourselves. That unchanged face, where we are not wearing a mask, when we are being our true selves without any filter. It must be pretty nice, since I haven't felt that way in a while.

"Everybody Wants to Rule the World" by Tears for Fears

As much as this bothers me to say, we do need someone here and there. Someone who worries, who cares. Someone to be there with you through every little tear, every lazy Friday night, someone to share that hot cocoa with mini marshmallows. Someone to remind you that you are not alone. Maybe it's not needed. Maybe I just really, really want it.

I am loved
by quite a few.
Through our
love and lust,
despite this uncanny love,
we must be worlds apart
for eternity.
There are forces in the way, pressing against the heart,
creating a questionable tension between the two of you
manifesting nothing but

At the moment I find it hard to believe that I know
what love really means
or what it's supposed to mean.
That's why I'm lost.

Once I met someone. Meeting him felt

I mean I found myself through his eyes, and his
beautiful crooked smile. Through our weird
conversations through our similarities.

a permanent scar.

extraordinary.

INNER THOUGHT #6

Sometimes you just meet people. People who have a massive impact on you. I believe that there are certain people who don't stick around for life, but their effects do. There are also soulmates; people with whom you form an unconditional connection. It can be a friend, or if you are just lucky enough, it can be the love of your life.

I still don't believe in happy endings, but I believe in happiness. I believe that one day, we'll all find that place that we are truly, madly, deeply, really *happy*. From the bottom of our hearts. We would have someone to share life with, to *live* with. There would be no empty promises.

Empty promises; broken promises. I've had my fair share of those, followed by goodbyes. After a while, your eyes become as dry as a desert in mid-July. Life becomes a series of unfortunate frustrations. People experience different things in life, everybody goes through so much. But for sure there are some that have it much easier than others. Words can fail; it happens almost every day. All the parents that forget about their children because they're busy with work. All the friends that forget about the ones who used to be part of their lives. All because forgetting, ignoring and pretending is less effort than being truthful about our feelings and emotions.

It's like ignorance has become a defence mechanism. We'd rather crawl under the seat than face our fears. I used to be like that, I still am sometimes. I'd rather hide from the problem than face it. The simple fact is that humans are allowed to make mistakes, they only become untrustworthy when they don't learn from them. Face the fact that if you actually love someone, you will find it in your heart to close your eyes on their mistakes and not only to forgive them for the mistakes but to forget about it. But the world is not as simple as that.

There's that moment in life when you're randomly sitting on your couch and trying to get your act together. And your favourite song plays on that random Spotify playlist and in that questionable moment with tears in your eyes.

There are also moments where you just get an epiphany. When you're reading a book while sitting at Starbucks siping on your chai tea latte, and you just see what you want, what you need. But you still don't know how to get there without changing yourself. Without ruining your structure. Without breaking a single brick that you are made of. You just sit there and question the truth of better tomorrow, the happily ever after, and much more.

I am complicated

There are always complications in everything and
anything.
It all relates to yourself,
the way you see the world,

the way you wake up
one morning and just feel happy.
That's what they all say, isn't it?
"Fake it 'til you make it?"
I question my existence
on a day to day basis -
every step I take,
every move I make
will affect everything.
They teach us how to cut a large cake into pieces but
we never really learn what we're supposed to do with
the pieces of our broken hearts.
Yes, love is amazing,
love is wonderful,
yes, it's the best thing in the world.
But what if we aren't doing it right?
Because in this world full of
mystery and misery,
it's really hard to see
right from wrong.

"It's *complicated*"
has been my emotional status since forever,

most likely since tenth grade,
when my ex broke my heart by calling me it

I can't decide what I want anymore. I want to feel love,
and be loved and experience it
but I'm scared.

Scared of being left alone, scared of drowning in a lake
filled with all of my emotions, at a dark spooky nigh.

How come this beautiful, fascinating shape of feeling
turns into this dump of unfortunate and blindness filled
with lust?

complicated

I think I might just be done.
Done struggling through these unfortunate events,
because day after day,
I'm just turning into a mess.

Sometimes I'm as lost as a kid in a

candy shop.

Day Number Twelve

Today, you didn't show up. I don't really know why but I was expecting you to show up. Maybe because you promised. But I think I should be okay with broken promises by now.

I really don't know if it's my high expectations or my high hopes or if you're just being a little bummer.

Thinking about it, you really are being a little irritating me right now. I think I know why you don't want a relationship through. It's because you

don't want to miss out on all the *good* things, isn't it? I've been there, babe.

You don't want to feel weighed down and stuck in one promising thing when you can have more. Well, you could be wrong.

Or at least you're wrong about me... because with the right person, I would make the greatest girlfriend. I would never stop you from hanging out with your friends and partying, even with girls. I might be a little jealous deep down that someone besides me is making you laugh, but I would never tell you that.

Also, I would never be worried that you would cheat on me or anything, because I would fully trust you.

I would be the astonishing girlfriend who would buy fancy whiskey on your birthday, open champagne every time you succeed in something (even the little things) and drink cheap red wine with you every lazy Sunday.

I would be the one who urges you to be the best version of yourself and who would never let you give up on your dreams; however big, however small.

> I would never let you settle until you are living your best life.

> > > Don't mix things up, babe!

If you find and love the right person,
if you let yourself to truly love and adore someone,

> you would absolutely want them to be there for you every second of every day.

To partake in all the exceptional moments,

> all the adventures,
> all the misery,
> all the love and
> all the happiness...

Life is filled with seriously unpleasant portions. And if you're in it alone, you will feel lonely, sad, depressed, and dark.

The ones that truly love you,

> who truly care about you,

are the lights illuminating your way through the darkness? They are true happiness, the ones that make you feel at home.

Maybe you didn't see me as one, or maybe this wasn't meant to be.

But I sadly still believe in love, and I am still hopeful that everyone has that one true person, to love and to cherish, and to call home.

I just hoped for you to be mine, because I'm fed up with doing this alone.

The Sunflower

There you are.
Standing there
        looking cute and humble.
                Looking so much more
        endearing than usual.
You usually show up quite early being sweet.
There's that warmth
        in your figure,
                in your perfect smile.
I never get to like someone,
                truly like someone –
        I never get a chance.
                Weirdly,
there's always someone else.
   Someone smarter,
                prettier,
who ends up being the perfect match.
                It's weird
how you can be in a crowd
        but still think of
                that someone
who's stuck in your mind.

"I'm a sunflower, a little funny.
        If I were a rose,
                maybe you'd want me..."

INNER THOUGHT #8.

The first day
after you left -
I can never forget it.
I was in bed,
shaking,
trying to wrap my head
around the idea
that you won't be here anymore.
I was upset
with myself,
for having trusting you,
for being vulnerable.
It was hard
getting over you,
over your broken promises,

over the hole you left
forever in my heart.

And yet, I'm thankful.
Because if you hadn't left,
I would never come

to love & to care

for the person I saw in the mirror

day after day.

You made me build walls so high
that no human could ever wreck them.

From the bottom of my heart

I've reached that level of independency

where

I don't even need myself anymore.

And the Sun Will Still Rise

"Life of the Party" by Shawn Mendes

Sometimes you need to take
the hardest fall.
You need to break into million pieces,
get shattered,
heck, even lose a couple of pieces,
just to find yourself.
I remember once I read in a biology textbook

that one time I actually read it,
that sometimes scientists smash DNA
into millions of pieces
and then try to match random pieces together to make
a new version of DNA.
Likewise, sometimes one needs to

                            w

                              r

                                  e

                                      c

                                        k

lose the mistaken chunks,
retain the fine ones.
All this
just to make a superior version of themselves - an
upgraded one.

What about people?
Well, if you ever,
in this heart-shattering journey,
met even one right soul,

be proud.
To some that are not good for you,
you need to say adios,
and those goodbyes will help you grow.

 Growth is not necessarily gaining something;

losing something can also help you to grow.
Sometimes people are meant to be
only memories.
I'm no expert, I'm just a person,
a person who writes

from time to time.
A person who is in
pain
that is "consuming all the air from my lungs,

ripping off all the skin from my bones".

A pain that could be just
a figment of my imagination

yet all this pain conceives

fear.

The fear of change,
fear that everyone will leave one day. Fear that
promises break
when you have that feeling of loss, feeling of
loneliness,
feeling of nonacceptance.

Then the thoughts sway constantly.
Sway constantly between right and wrong.

Unclear questions
going around in your head
accelerate to every inch of your body.
Now you're filled with anxiety,
a mocked-up feeling
that is probably only in your head.
You get up,
look in the mirror
and maybe for just one moment,
you see the real you.
I'm no expert,
just a person who writes.
But I know this;
the sun will always

r i s e

a g a i n

INNER THOUGHT #9
"Someone You Love" by Lewis Capaldi

So, twenty years have passed by, and to be honest I've grown so much that it's simply impossible to believe. I turned a new leaf and found great values in life for both love and loss.

I learnt that when you trust the right people, you will discover great friendships. In my experience, they've brought me wonderful memories that I wouldn't change for the world. And I learnt that it's okay to let people see the worst in you, because if they're the right people for you, they will stay no matter how dark the nights will get.

I learnt that I'm a beautiful, powerful woman who is worthy of the love I'm looking for - good things simply just take time. Just like this book! I've changed so much since the very first word I typed out on my laptop.

I learnt that as you grow up, you start to lose the "fake" and instead start to gain faith.

Faith in life and its beauty. Faith in the love that everyone around you is willing to give you, *unconditionally*. Most importantly, faith in yourself.

You, with the broken bits and all the imperfections that make you perfect. You will come to a level of self-fulfillment to accept yourself as the person that you truly are. As beautiful as you are as seen in the eyes of others.

It's very hard. But not impossible. And through all that you do, never forget that there is always room for more growth.

Always and forever,
Nafas

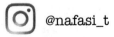 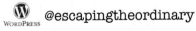